Mel Bay's

CLASSICAL GUITAR POSITION STUDIES

by Walt Lawry

Visit us on the Web at www.melbay.com — E-mail us at email@melbay.com

INTRODUCTION

This book is designed to acquaint the classical guitar student with the concept of playing music in different positions along the neck of the guitar.

Each position is handled separately. The material in each position includes a display of the available notes, an exercise, and a number of study pieces presented according to their ease of playing. Many of the pieces are played entirely in the study position, others require position shifts. The positions used are given in the introductory notes for each piece.

Complete left hand fingerings are supplied for each piece of music. Students should be familiar with music in the first position before starting these studies.

TABLE OF CONTENTS

POSITIONS

Positions are the various places along the neck of the guitar where you can place your left hand. Positions are named for the fret on which the index finger plays. If the index finger is on the first fret, then you are in first position. The other three fingers are responsible for the next three frets. For example, in ninth position the index finger plays the ninth fret, the middle finger plays the tenth fret, the ring finger plays the eleventh fret, and the little finger plays the twelfth fret.

The thumb of the left hand should always be placed directly opposite the fingers. It should never drag behind them on the neck. For most hands, the best place for the thumb is opposite the fret played by the middle finger. Here it can support the action of all the fingers.

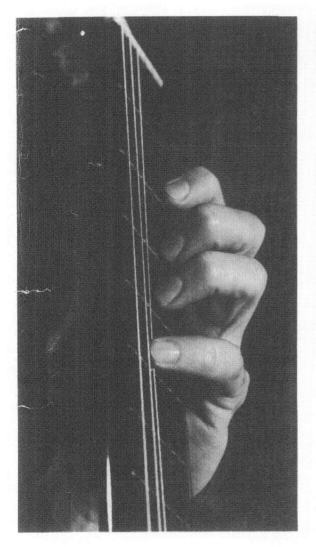

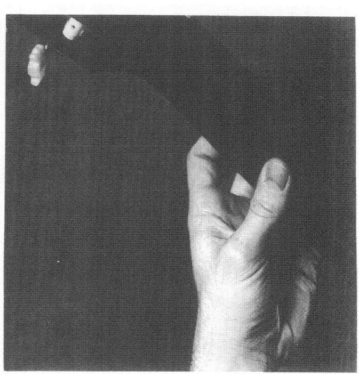

CORRECT

CORRECT

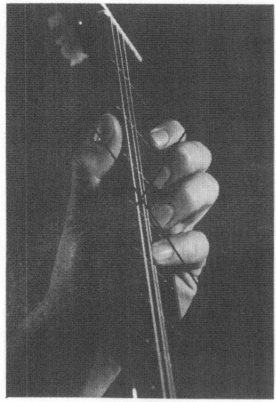
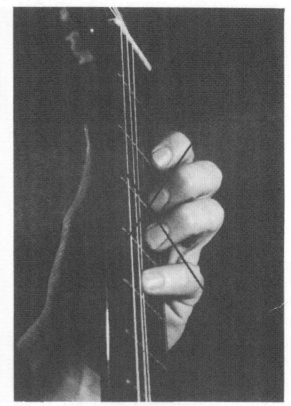

INCORRECT   INCORRECT

Positions are indicated by Roman numerals.

I   = first position
II   = second position
III = third position
IV   = fourth position
V   = fifth position
VI   = sixth position
VII = seventh position
VIII = eighth position
IX   = ninth position

These are the positions covered by this book.

Barres are indicated by the letter "C" followed by a Roman numeral showing the fret where the index finger is to play the barre. Partial barres are indicated by a fraction giving the precise number of strings to be barred by the index finger.

1/3 C = two strings barred
1/2 C = three strings barred
2/3 C = four strings barred
5/6 C = five strings barred

Occasionally you will have to play a note that is one fret higher or lower than the frets covered by the position you are in. These notes are generally played by stretching the first or fourth finger out of position to reach the necessary fret. The rest of the hand stays in normal position. This is called an extension. If a study calls for extensions, they will be brought to your attention in the introductory notes.

SHIFTING

Shifting is the process of moving from one position to another along the neck of the guitar. Shifting is a three-part process, as follows:

1. Release all pressure in the left hand.
2. Move the hand along the neck to the new position.
3. Play the new notes.

It is very important to relax the hand when shifting.

There are three types of shifts, as discussed below.

OPEN STRING SHIFT

This is a type of shift where you play an open string right at the moment of shifting. This is perhaps the easiest shift to do, since the open string gives you a little extra time to move your hand to the new position.

GUIDE FINGER SHIFT

This is a type of shift where the last note of the old position and the first note of the new position are played by the same finger on the same string. An example will make this clear.

The second finger can "guide" the hand to the new position. Be sure to release the pressure on the guide finger when changing positions to make the shift as noiseless as possible. Guide finger shifts are indicated by a straight line connecting the guide finger notes.

FREE SHIFT

This type of shift has neither open strings to give you extra time nor guide fingers to help position your hand. Free shifts tend to be the most challenging to learn.

The types of shifts required for each piece are given in its introductory notes.

2nd
POSITION

NOTES IN SECOND POSITION

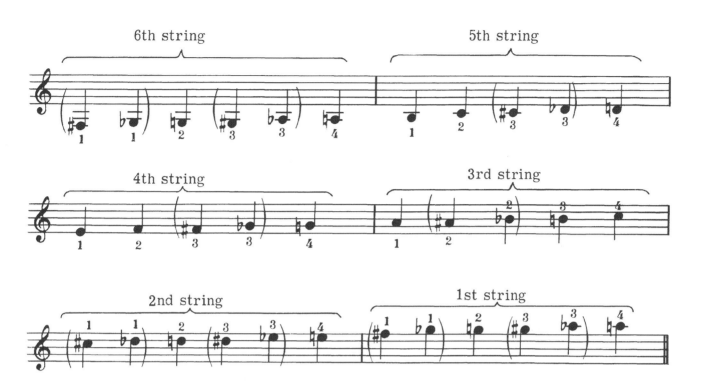

II

EXERCISE

M. Carcassi Op. 59

VALSE

Position II

F. Sor Op. 48 No. 4

MINUETTO

Positions used: I, II

Shifts: Open string.

Be sure to relax the left hand when shifting. Make certain the thumb moves
right along with the rest of the hand; don't let it drag along the back of the
neck. The open string shifts allow you a little extra time to move your hand to the
new position.

F. Sor Op. 44 No. 14

MINUET OP. 48

Positions used: I, II

Shifts: Open string, guide finger, and free.

This piece requires more frequent position changes than the preceeding Minuetto. It is part of a Minuet and three Variations. The variations are included in the appropriate parts of this book. They can be found as follows:

Variation I   - fifth position, pg. 43.
Variation II - third position, pg. 20.
Variation III - ninth position, pg. 77.

F. Sor

ALLEGRETTO

Positions used: I, II

Shifts: Open string, guide finger, and free.

M. Giuliani Op. 9

14

3rd
POSITION

NOTES IN THIRD POSITION

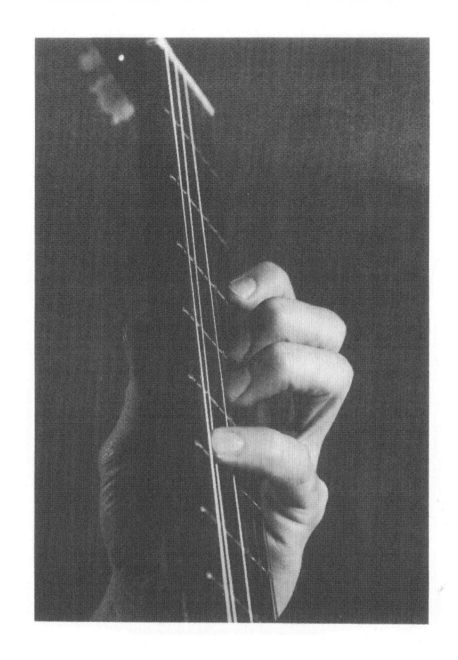

III

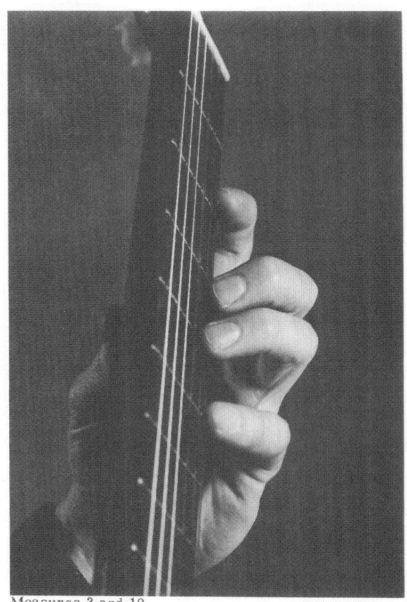

Measures 3 and 19

EXERCISE

In this exercise, the F-sharps in measures 3 and 19 are not found in normal third position. The index finger of the left hand is cocked back to the second fret in order the play these notes. The rest of the hand remains in third position. This reaching out of normal position for an occasional note is called an extension.

F. Sor Op. 60

MINUET OP. 48
VARIATION NO. 2

Positions used: I, III

Shifts: Open string

F. Sor

20

VALSE

Positions used: I, II, III

Shifts: Open string, guide finger, and free.

<u>Valse</u> contains a number of slurs. Performing slurs sometimes puts tension in the left hand, making shifts more difficult. If this happens to you, try omitting the slurs until you have learned the piece well. Then go back and add them in.

F. Sor Op. 51 No. 5

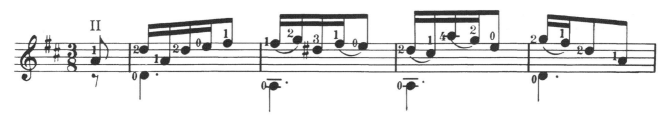

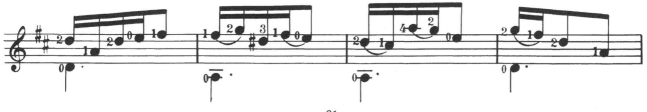

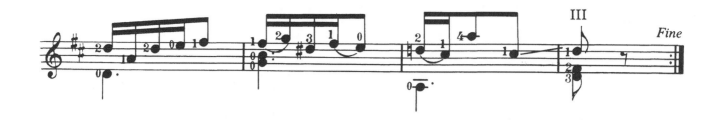

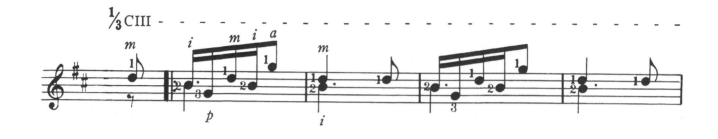

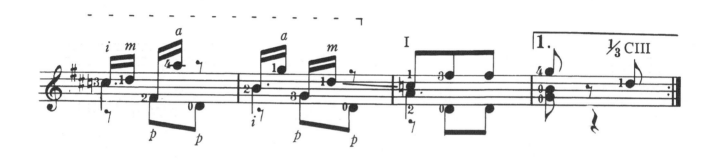

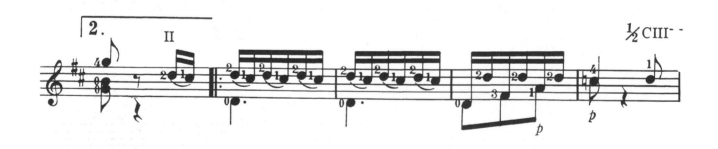

22

LARGHETTO

Positions used: I, II, III

Shifts: Guide finger and free.

M. Giuliani Op. 30 No. 17

ANDANTE

Positions used: I, II, III

Shifts: Guide finger and free.

Leave your first finger down for the entire length of the first measure. It will then act as a guide finger for the following shift. The first finger extends one fret lower than normal in measure 12.

F. Sor Op. 57

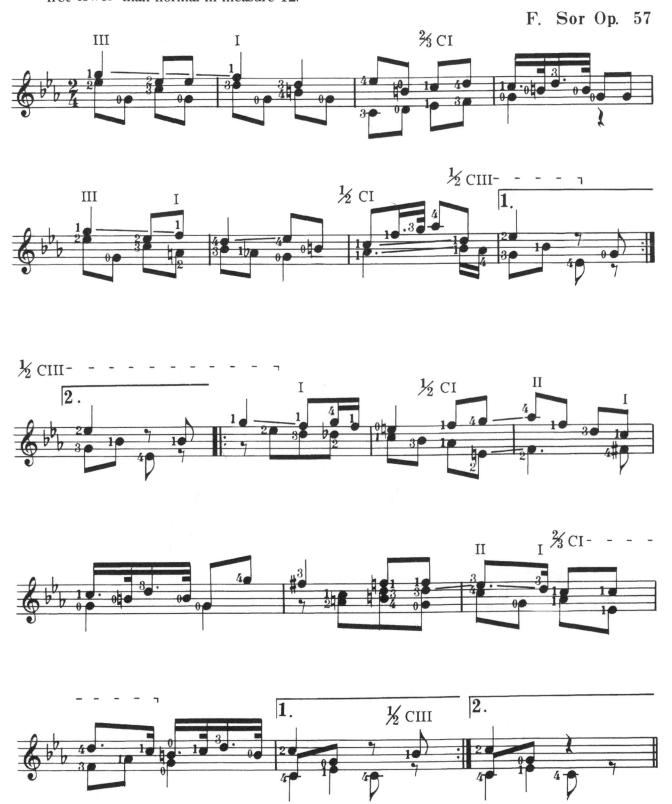

24

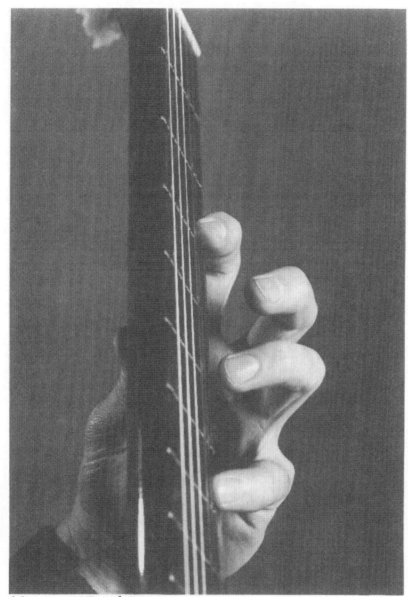

Measures 17 and 21 —page 26

ALLEGRETTO

Positions used: I, II, III

Shifts: Open string, guide finger, and free.

<u>Allegretto</u> contains two left hand extensions. There is a downward extension using the first finger in measures 9 and 11, and there is an upward extension using the fourth finger in measures 17 and 21.

F. Sor Op. 1 No. 2

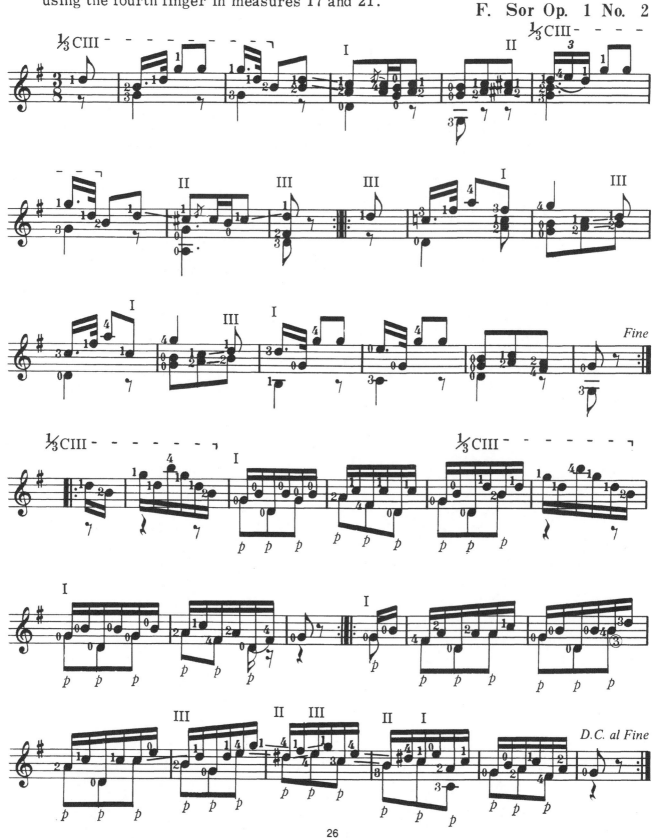

4th
POSITION

NOTES IN FOURTH POSITION

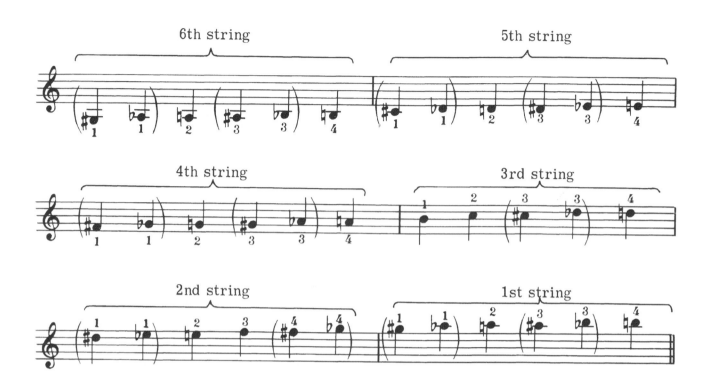

28

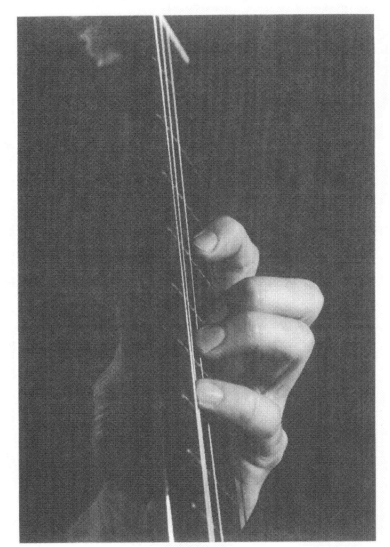

EXERCISE

M. Carcassi Op. 59

WALTZ

Position IV

M. Carcassi Op. 59

THEME AND VARIATION

Position IV

M. Carcassi Op. 11 No. 10

Variation

32

VALZER

Positions used: I, IV

Shifts: Guide finger.

F. Carulli Op. 80 No. 5

VALSE

Positions used: I, II, IV

Shifts: Open string and guide finger.

<u>Valse</u> requires constant use of the fourth finger and may take a little longer to learn. Eliminate slurs if they cause problems but add them later when you are more familiar with the piece.

F. Sor Op. 57 No. 1

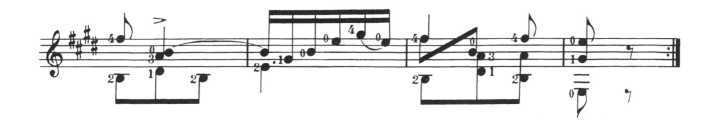

½ CI - - - - - - - - - - - - - - - - - - -

½ CI   IV

I

D.C. al Fine

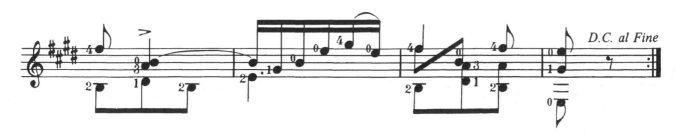

5th
POSITION

NOTES IN FIFTH POSITION

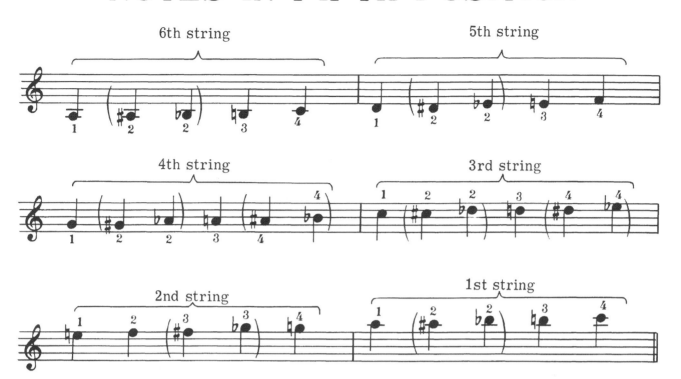

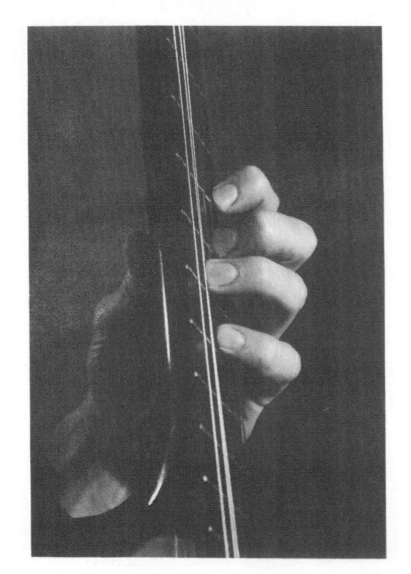

EXERCISE

M. Carcassi Op. 59

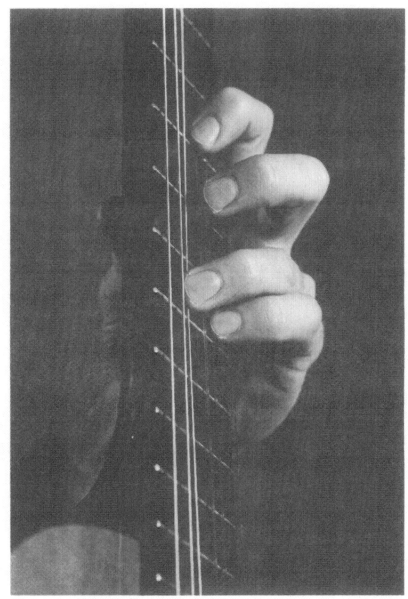

Measures 6 and 12 —page 40

POCO ALLEGRETTO

This piece is played entirely in fifth position. There are two extensions. In measures 6 and 12 the third finger extends upward one fret. In measure 11 the first finger extends downward one fret.

F. Carulli

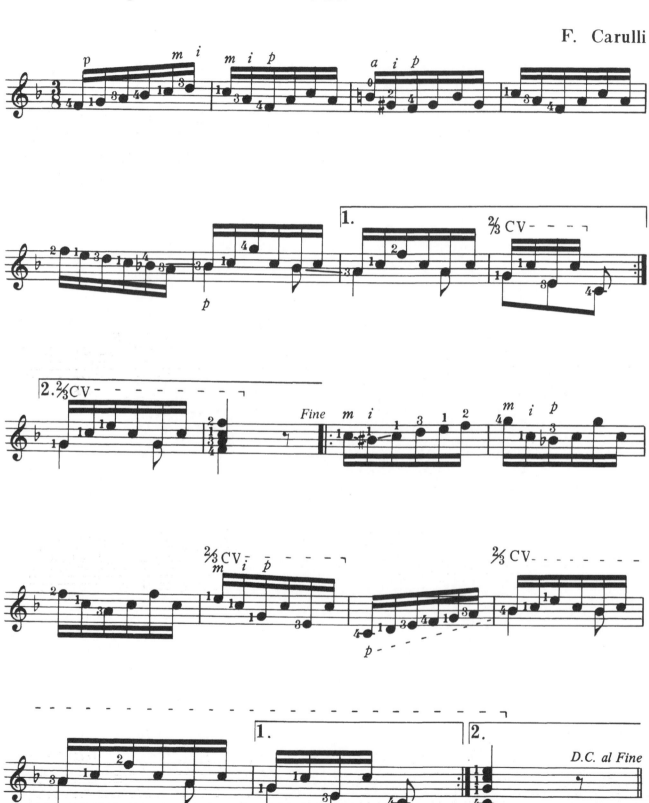

VALSE

Position V

M. Carcassi Op. 3 No. 2

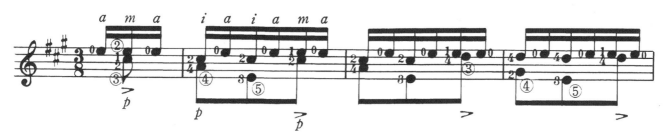

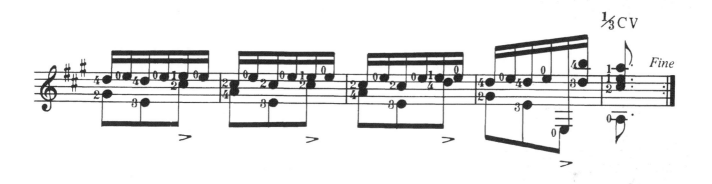

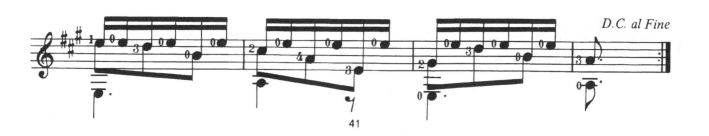

ANDANTE AGITATO

Positions used: I, II, V

Shifts: Guide finger and free.

F. Carulli Op. 211 No. 12

MINUET OP. 48
VARIATION I

Positions used: I, II, IV, V

Shifts: Open string and free.

This piece uses an upward extension in fifth position in measure 11.

F. Sor

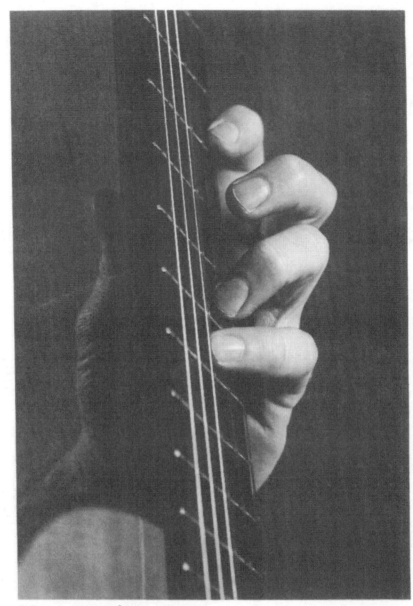

Measures 1 and 29

ALLEGRETTO

Positions used: I, II, III, IV, V

Shifts: Guide finger and free.

There is an upward extension of both the third and fourth fingers in measures 1 and 29. Be sure to follow all of the fingerings carefully in this piece.

F. Sor Op. 35 No. 11

6th
POSITION

NOTES IN SIXTH POSITION

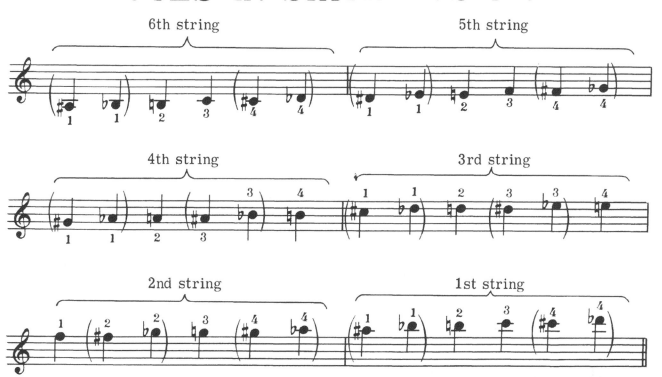

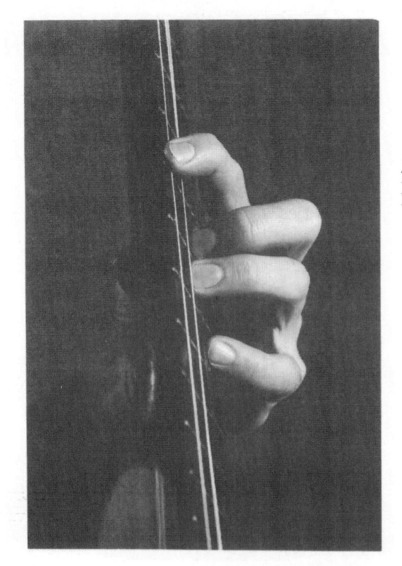

EXERCISE

48

ALLEGRETTO

Positions used: I, VI

Shifts: Open string.

In measures 4 and 12 of this Allegretto, the B-sharps are played by extending the first finger downward.

M. Giuliani Op. 147 No. 6

WALTZ

Positions used: II, V, VI

Shifts: Open string and guide finger.

Look for upward extensions in measures 1, 5, 13, and 14. There is a downward extension in measure 4.

F. Sor Op. 13 No. 2

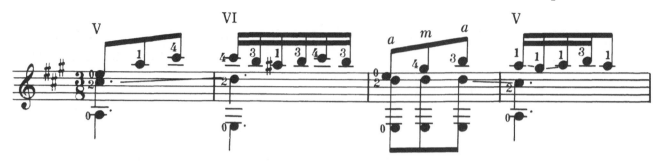

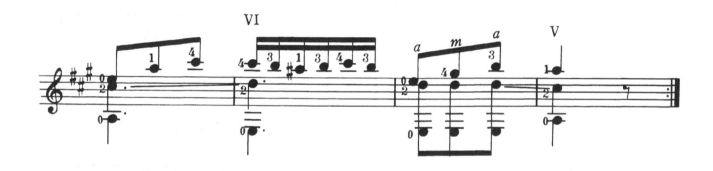

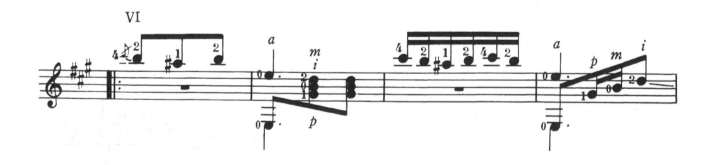

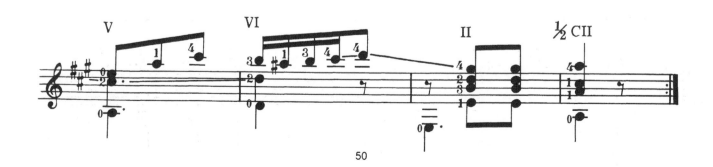

LESSON XXII

Positions used: I, II, III, VI

Shifts: Guide finger and free.

F. Sor Op. 31

Tempo di marcia
Moderato

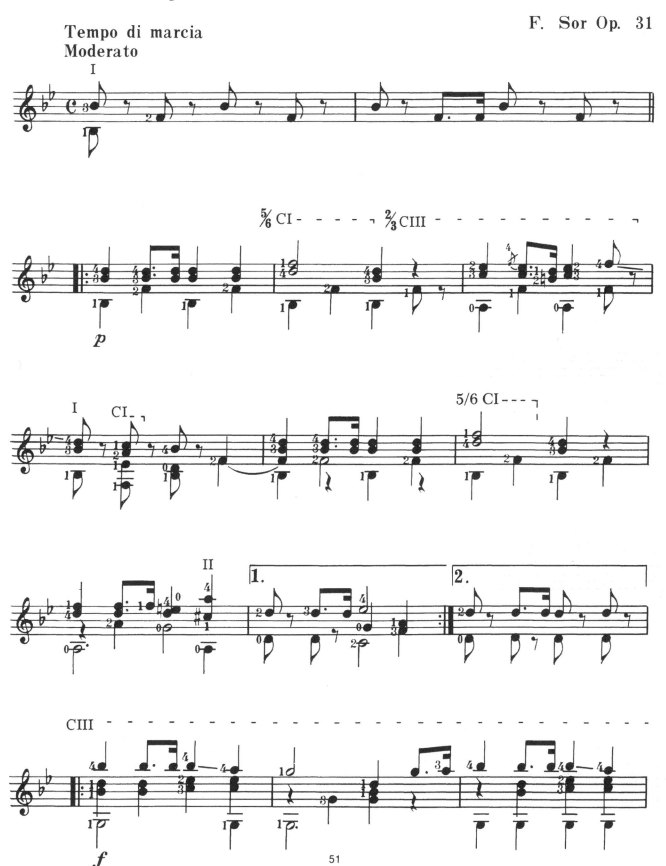

51

7th
POSITION

NOTES IN SEVENTH POSITION

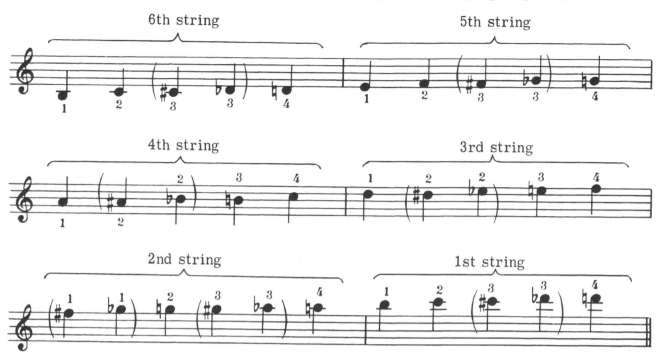

EXERCISE

M. Carcassi Op. 59

ALLEGRETTO

Position VII

M. Carcassi Op. 59

56

VIVACE

Positions used: I, II, V, VII

Shifts: Open string, guide finger, and free.

M. Giuliani Op. 100 No. 19

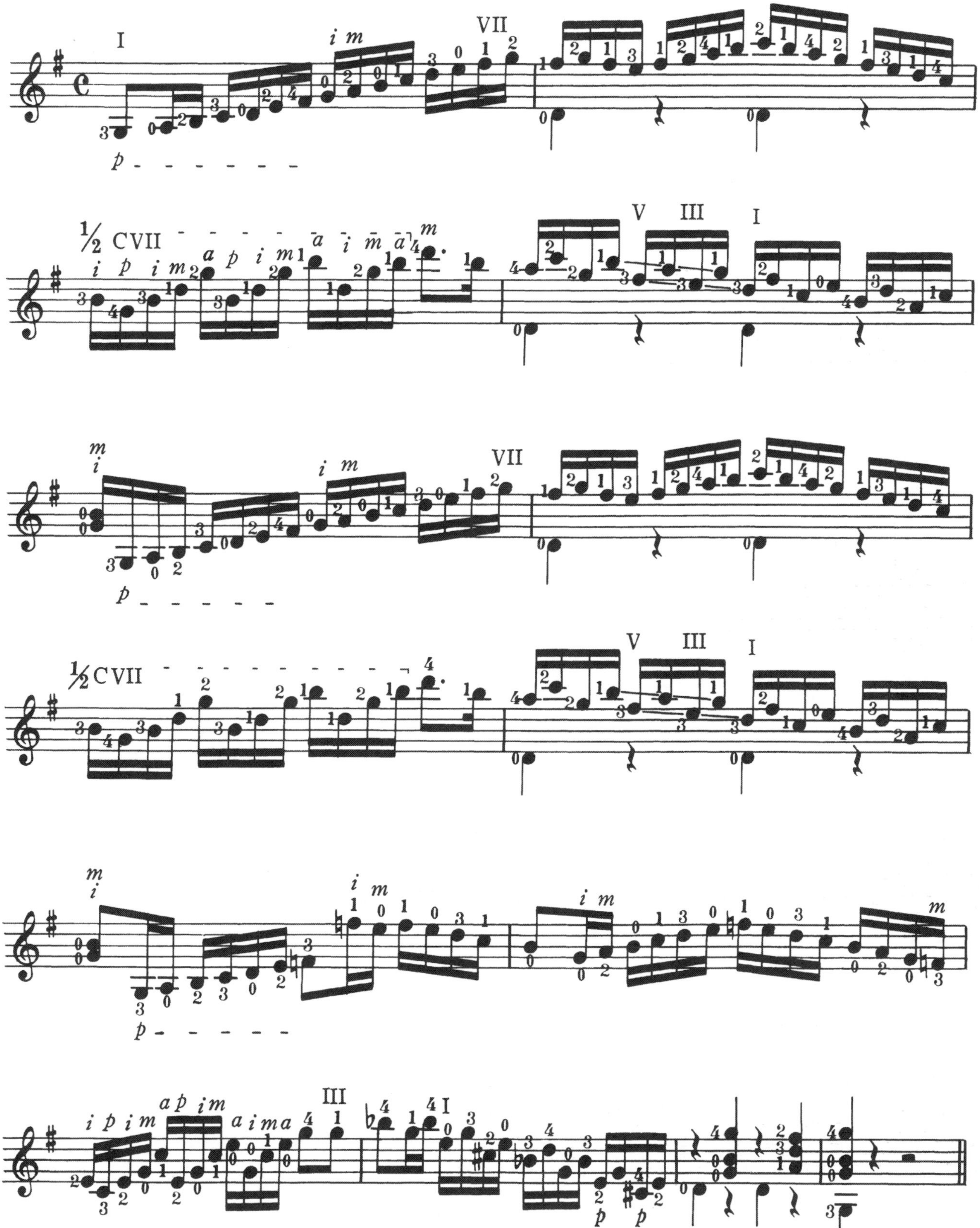

ALLEGRETTO

Positions used: I, II, V, VII

Shifts: Open string and free.

M. Carcassi Op. 59

ALLEGRETTO

Positions used: I, II, IV, VII

Shifts: Open string and free.

This Allegretto is based on a theme from the opera William Tell by Gioaccino Rossini.

M. Carcassi Op. 36

MINUETTO

Positions used: I, II, III, IV, V, VII

Shifts: Guide finger and free.

F. Sor Op. 25

Allegro

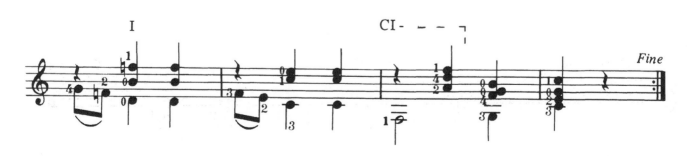

Trio

63

8th
POSITION

NOTES IN EIGHTH POSITION

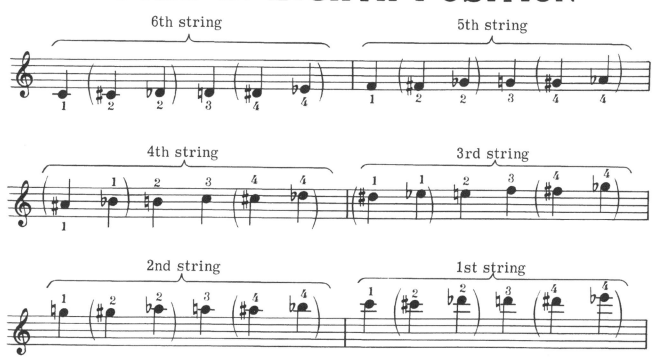

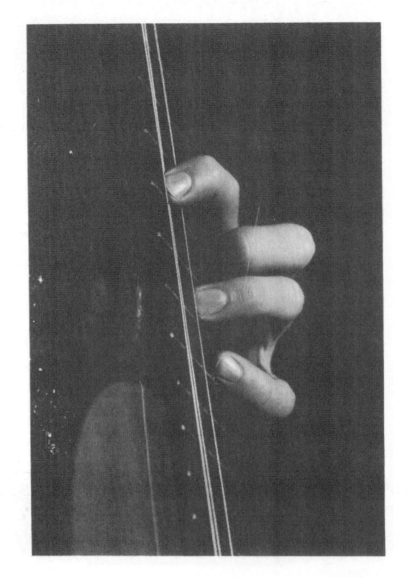

EXERCISE

ADAGIO

Positions used: I, II, III, VIII

Shifts: Open string, guide finger, and free.

In measure 6 of this <u>Adagio</u> the B-natural and the E-natural are played with an upward extension of the fourth finger.

M. Giuliani Op. 7

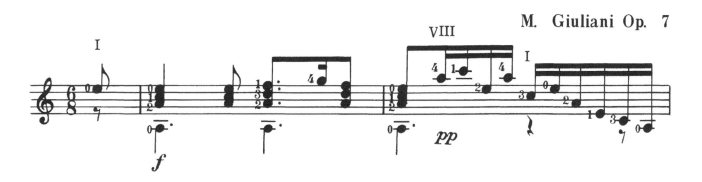

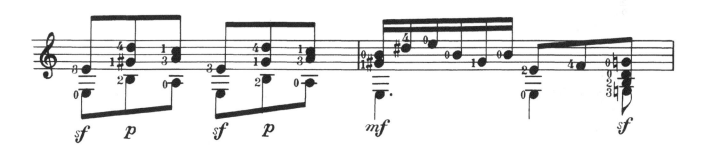

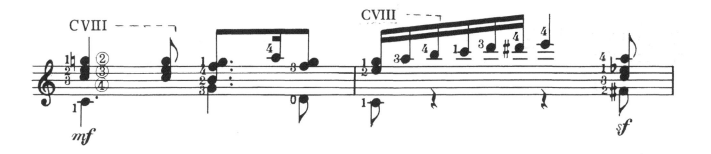

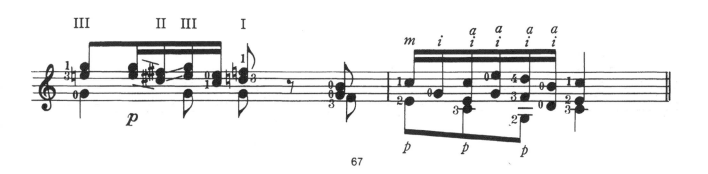

MODERATO

Positions used: I, II, IV, V, VII, VIII

Shifts: Open string and guide finger.

N. Coste

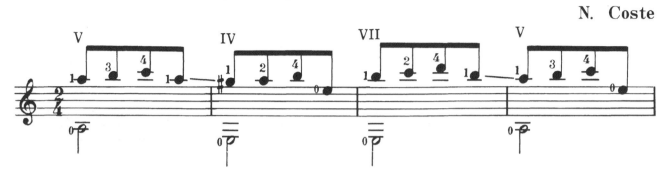

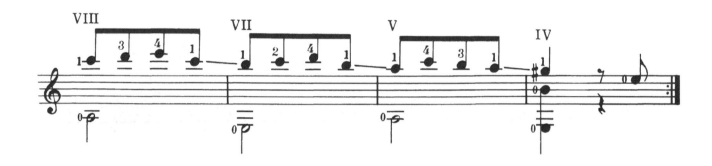

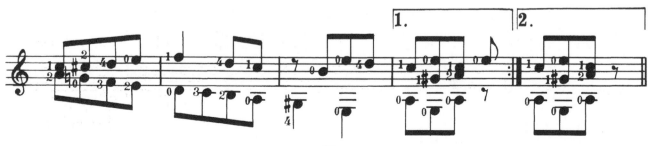

ALLEGRO

Positions used: I, II, III, VI, VIII

Shifts: Open string, guide finger, and free.

N. Coste

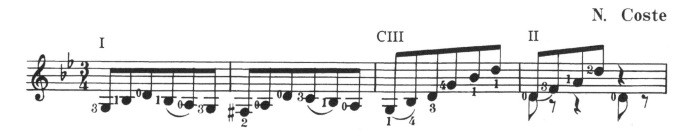

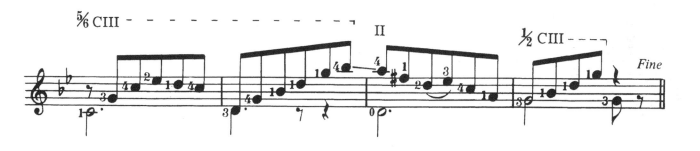

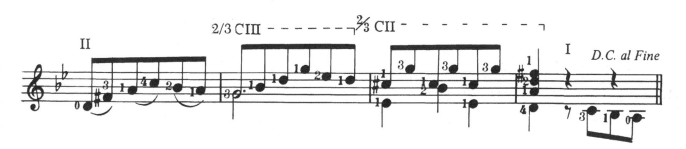

WALTZ

Positions used: I, II, III, VIII

Shifts: Open string, guide finger, and free.

<u>Waltz</u> has an upward extension in measure 21.

F. Sor Op. 17 No. 6

9th
POSITION

NOTES IN NINTH POSITION

EXERCISE

M. Carcassi Op. 59

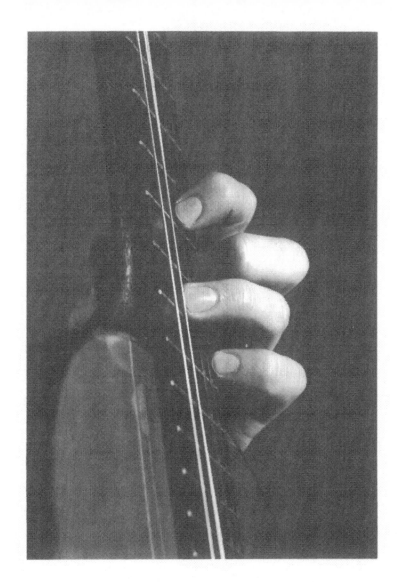

ALLEGRETTO

Position IX

M. Giuliani Op. 147 No. 11

MODERATO

Positions used: I, II, VII, IX

Shifts: Open string and free.

M. Giuliani Op. 38

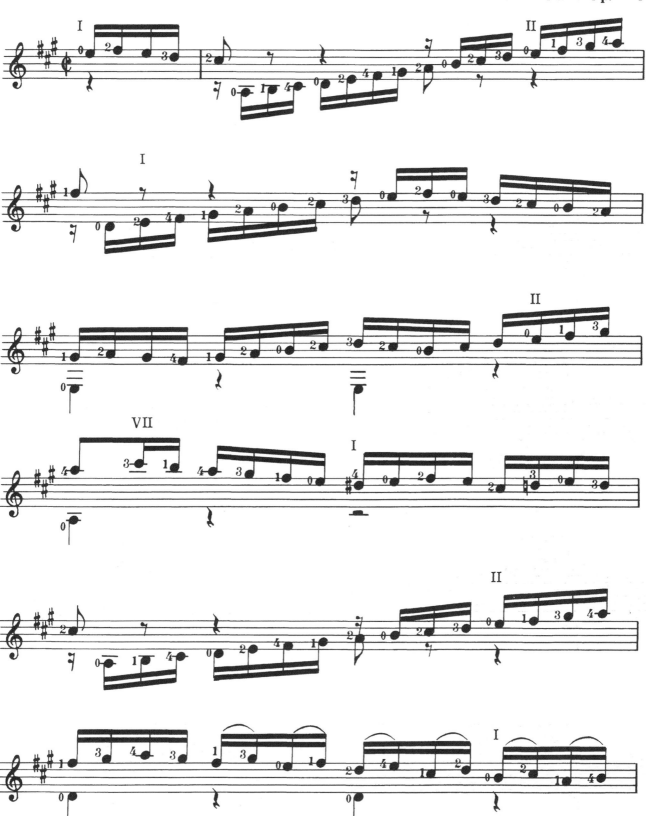

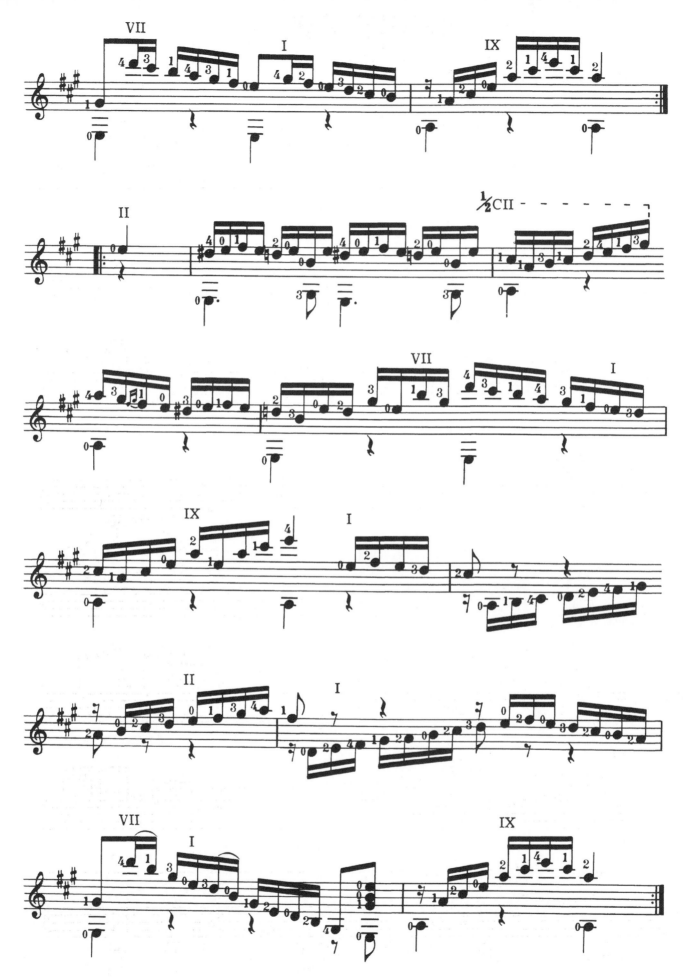

MINUET OP. 48
VARIATION 3

Positions used: I, II, IV, V, IX

Shifts: Open string and guide finger.

F. Sor

ALLEGRETTO

Positions used: I, II, V, VII, IX

Shifts: Open string, guide finger, and free.

M. Giuliani Op. 147 No. 5

79

ALLEGRO

Positions used: I, II, IV, V, VII, IX

Shifts: Open string and guide finger.

This Allegro comes from the same group of pieces as Carcassi's Allegretto
Op. 36 which is found in the seventh position studies.
Allegro is based on the overture to William Tell.

M. Carcassi Op. 36

ANDANTINO GRAZIOSO

Positions used: I, II, IV, VI, VII, IX

Shifts: Open string, guide finger, and free.

M. Carcassi Op. 59 No. 40

ANDANTINO

Positions used: I, II, III, IV, V, VII, IX

Shifts: Open string, guide finger, and free.

M. Carcassi Op. 60 No. 3

Everybody's Music Teacher

Printed in Great Britain
by Amazon.co.uk, Ltd.,
Marston Gate.